IMITATE GOD
AND GET RESULTS

BILL WINSTON

Unless otherwise noted, all scripture quotations are taken from the King James Version of the Bible.

Imitate God and Get Results
ISBN 1-59544-117-4
Copyright © 2005 Bill Winston
Bill Winston Ministries
P.O. Box 947
Oak Park, Illinois 60303-0947

Cover & Interior design by Jerrold Daniels

Printed in the United States of America. All rights reserved under International Copyright Law. Contents and/or cover may not be reproduced in whole or part in any form without the express written consent of the Publisher.

CONTENTS

INTRODUCTION
i

CHAPTER ONE
HOW GOD CREATED YOU – FOR DOMINION
1

CHAPTER TWO
LIVING FROM THE INSIDE OUT
Developing the Right Image of Yourself
9

CHAPTER THREE
PRACTICING THE GOD-KIND OF FAITH
25

CHAPTER FOUR
YES, YOU CAN DO MIRACLES
39

CONCLUSION
45

INTRODUCTION

Do you realize that we are living in the last days – the days Paul called "perilous times" in his second letter to Timothy?

As believers, God has entrusted us with an awesome responsibility. We are the "harvesting generation" that must reclaim all the wealth of the wicked that has been laid up for the just (Proverbs 13:22), the wealth that's needed to complete God's plan of redemption by bringing the Gospel to every nation.

To do this, we have to operate the same way God operates – with His power, with His anointing, with His faith, with His love, and by speaking His Word. We are His children, joint-heirs with His Son, Jesus, and we have been given that ability.

The purpose of this book is to show you how, by God's grace and the power of the Holy Spirit within you, you can operate like God, even in the midst of perilous times, and come out on top. Let me show you how to imitate God and get results.

CHAPTER ONE

HOW GOD CREATED YOU - FOR DOMINION

Things are happening fast these days. The earth is reeling under a curse, the curse that was brought on by Adam. Ever since Adam fell, sinful man has been sowing to the flesh, and the earth has been reaping corruption. Now judgment is coming on the land.

However, you and I have been chosen by God to live in this time. Like Queen Esther, we were ***"born for such a time as this."*** God not only had us born now, but born again and equipped with what it takes to overcome the world by using our faith.

For whatsoever is born of God overcometh the world: and this is the

> *victory that overcometh the world, even our faith.*
>
> *(I John 5:4)*

We are here to fulfill what I call the Dominion Mandate. It's the mandate that God gave to Adam way back in Genesis 1. After God had created the earth, light, day and night, etc., He created man.

> *And God said, Let us make man in our own image, after our likeness: and let them have dominion over the fish of the sea, and over the fowl of the air and over the cattle, and over all the earth, and over every creeping thing that creepeth upon the earth.*
>
> *(Genesis 1:26)*

I want you to notice one thing. What God expected Adam and mankind to do was to have dominion over this earth. Now having dominion means to rule, to govern, to subdue, or to manage.

God made the earth for man. He expected Adam, and those of us who came after him, to exercise stewardship and ownership – to take care of the earth for God. We were meant to be in charge here. That was God's plan, and He never changes His plan.

Adam was supposed to rule the earth. He was created in God's image after God's likeness. God didn't say, "Let us have dominion." He said, ***"Let them have dominion."*** "Them" was Adam and Eve. So, as Adam's descendants, we're the ones who are to have dominion.

It's also important to know that God first created Adam as a spirit. He didn't form his body until Genesis 2:7. God is a spirit, Adam was a spirit, and you are a spirit, first of all.

You live in your body, but the reason you are in God's image and His likeness is that you were created as a spirit. Your body is just your house while you're on the earth.

The reason the Church hasn't been dominating the earth and our circumstances as we should have, is that most of us haven't realized who we are. It hasn't been taught.

Man's Reconnection to God

Before Adam sinned, he had a direct line of communication with God through his spirit. God constantly gave him revelation knowledge. That's how Adam was able to name all of the animals. He was connected to God and he was walking in faith and fellowship with God. He perceived what God thought.

Once he sinned, that connection was broken. He had to go from revelation to information - what he could receive through his five senses. Jesus came to restore that God connection for us, so that we could walk in revelation knowledge, as God always had planned.

After you were born again, you became reconnected to God. You learned from the Word how to walk by faith and you started to receive revelation knowledge, to see things you couldn't see before.

What you were doing was seeing through the eye of faith. Faith sees the invisible. When you're walking in the flesh, walking only in sense knowledge, you have to depend on information. You process information with your natural ability. You reason with your logical mind, and that's limited, no matter how much education you have.

Not one ounce of faith comes out of your head. Faith comes from the spirit, or the heart, alone. When Adam lost his connection to God's revelation knowledge, he had to operate in the intellectual realm, on head knowledge.

Let me stress what being made in the image and likeness of God really means – for Adam and for us. It means we are made to act just like God.

We're Made Like God

We are made to walk just like God, by faith and not by sight. We're made to talk just like God, *"calling things that be not as though they were."* We're made to see just like God, looking not at the things that are seen, but at the things that are not seen.

We also are made to think just like God. In the natural, that just isn't possible, as it says in Isaiah 55:8-9, *"For my thoughts are not your thoughts, neither are your ways my ways, saith the Lord. For as the heavens are higher than the earth, so are my ways higher than your ways, and my thoughts than your thoughts."* But once we're born again, God wants us to come on back up and think like He does.

That's strong stuff, but we've got to do it. You can't keep thinking, "I'm from Alabama" or "I'm from Iowa." That's just your body talking. Where you are from now is from God!

You were born out of the womb of the Holy Ghost. You were born of God and <u>created</u> in Christ Jesus for good works that He ordained before the foundation of the world – works you can do only with God's ability.

The world needs to see those good works, for we are in a time when the earth is reeling under some things that have been done, things that bring devastation. You see them in the form of sickness and disease, famine and pestilence. These are things that Jesus said will be indications of the last days.

However, we are to *"be of good cheer"* for Jesus has overcome the world, and so have we, when we operate in faith. ***"In the world ye shall have tribulation: but be of good cheer; I have overcome the world"*** (John 16:33).

Faith Dominates the Enemy

Our faith is the first thing the enemy wants to steal from us. Satan is coming after your faith because he knows that without it, you can only go as far as your natural ability can take you. And that's not far enough.

Without our faith working for us, we're limited to Satan's arena, *"such as is common to man."* And we cannot dominate him with information; he has access to all there is. We must have revelation.

Satan has to operate in the natural. Though he's a fallen spirit, he no longer can operate in the spirit realm. He cannot go up into that upper level where you can live. You can put him under your feet and keep him there. You have authority over him and over all his demon hosts as well.

CHAPTER TWO

LIVING FROM THE INSIDE OUT
DEVELOPING THE RIGHT IMAGE OF YOURSELF

Faith Dominates Fear

You need to develop your faith because the times are only getting harder. People, including a lot of church people, are filled with fear - fear of terrorists, fear of disease, fear of the weather. When the hurricanes hit Florida, lines of cars were scrambling to get out, almost bumper-to-bumper, and people were panicking. They couldn't get off the islands fast enough.

However, we're supposed to operate in faith, not fear. We have been made for such a time as this. God knew these would be hard times, and He knew that we could handle them.

To exercise our faith, we're going to have to start speaking some stuff. It's the only way to dominate. The world may not understand what you're saying because you're from another planet. You were born from above. And God wants to use you to show people that His Kingdom rules over everything.

We have to get back to where Adam was before he fell. Even though he was made in the image and likeness of God, when Adam sinned, his faith turned to fear, and his righteousness to unrighteousness. God's plan is to restore us; He wants us to take back everything the devil has stolen from the body of Christ. It's our inheritance, and we have to learn how to receive it.

Something to Meditate. God's plan was always for man to have dominion in the earth. We are to operate the same way He does – by speaking what we want into existence, by saying exactly what the Word of God says.

Faith Gets Your Needs Met from the Inside Out

While your inheritance and your provisions come from God, they come by faith, from the inside out. Though they come from God, they come through your spirit.

You were designed to operate just like God. And how does God operate? How did He create the earth, light, day and night, etc.? He spoke them into being! Where were they before they manifested? They were in God.

And that's how God wants you to operate. You never were meant to operate from the outside in. You always were meant to live from the inside out.

Just think about that. It changes everything, especially how you're thinking. If you're meant to live from the inside out, your provisions don't come from the outside, they come from the inside. That changes everything around you.

There is nothing around you that can keep you down or hold you back. Because if you want some more, all you have to do is speak some more.

Faith Operates from the Heart, not the Head

Jesus said to the father of the demon-possessed boy in Mark 9:23, *"If thou canst believe, all things are possible to him that believeth."*

And how do you believe? With your heart. You don't believe with your head. The head, the mind, only believes what it can see. It's designed that way. The head is not designed to see the invisible; the heart is.

Your head feeds off the senses – what it can see or feel. But your heart feeds off the Word. Whatever the Word says, your heart receives. Many times when you speak something in the

Word your head will go, "Tilt!" It won't receive it because to your head it's impossible.

Remember when Jesus came to the gravesite of Lazarus? Martha came up to Him first and said, (I'm paraphrasing) "Master, if you had been here earlier, my brother wouldn't have died." And Jesus answered her, ***"Thy brother shall rise again."***

She thought Jesus was speaking of the Last Day Resurrection. She couldn't get her mind around the idea that Jesus was going to raise up Lazarus then and there. And, let's be honest, you probably couldn't have either, if you'd been there.

Martha had heard Jesus preach about the resurrection and she believed in that. But she was looking at the current situation in the natural. There was a disconnect from her spirit. Her natural mind was thinking that Lazarus had been dead for four days and his body was starting to stink.

But, what Jesus really was saying to Martha was what God said to Moses way back in Exodus, **"I AM."** God has no future and no past. He's outside of time.

Faith Overrides Time Delays

When you're dealing with faith, you come out of time zones and go into the eternal. Martha was looking at time, but when you walk by faith, you can have dominion over time.

The Syrophenician woman who came to Jesus in Mark 7:26 had faith that moved Jesus out of time. Her daughter was sick at home and she wanted Jesus to heal her. But because she wasn't a Jew, she didn't have a covenant. Still, she persisted with her faith.

When Jesus told her He was sent only to the Jews (at that time), and not to the Gentiles, whom the Jews considered the same as dogs, the woman called Jesus "Lord" and said that even the dogs get the crumbs that fall under the table.

Seeing her great faith, Jesus stepped out of time and healed her daughter. What He did was give her the same blessing we have as Gentiles after the cross. He was responding to her and her faith as if she were under the New Covenant.

When you really have faith in God and His Word, all things become possible for you. It means that your heart is convinced. What you believe has changed you, glory to God!

Faith Draws from Heaven's Provisions

You know in your heart, in your spirit man, that God has a heavenly reservoir, or treasury, for you. Peter describes it this way, ***"According as his divine power hath given unto us all things that pertain unto life and godliness, through the knowledge of him that hath called us to glory and virtue"*** (2 Peter 1:3). God has already given us all things, and all things means that nothing is left out.

We started out talking about the perilous times we are in according to II Timothy 3:1. The Amplified Bible Translation calls them times that are ***"hard to deal with and hard to bear."*** And it's only going to get worse in the world's system.

But you and I are in the Kingdom of God – we're on the Kingdom system. We have been sent here as ambassadors to manifest God's will in this earth no matter what Satan has done or will do. We're here to manifest the Kingdom and to draw in people to be saved.

God Does Not Respond to Begging

We are not beggars. God does not respond to begging, He responds to faith. Look at the difference between two beggars we see in the New Testament.

The beggar Lazarus that Jesus talks about in Luke 16 sat daily at the gate of the rich man, begging and getting nothing. The rich man was living high, but Lazarus was crippled and immobile. He even had sores that the dogs came and licked.

Then this beggar died. Nowhere in the Bible does it say that he ever got his needs met. He died just as broke, and just as sick, too, even though he was the seed of Abraham. Do you know why he died broke? Because he was trying to beg God and <u>God doesn't respond to begging.</u>

Now let's look at another beggar - blind Bartimaeus in Mark 10. He was on the roadside when Jesus passed by. He knew Who Jesus was, and when he heard He was passing by he cried out, ***"Jesus, Thou Son of David, have mercy on me!"***

Jesus apparently kept walking, which caused Bartimaeus to yell louder. Those around him told him to shut up, but he just kept screaming and he got Jesus' attention. Jesus asked him to come, and Bartimaeus dropped his beggar's garment that he was required to wear and ran to Him.

Bartimaeus had faith. He knew he wasn't going to need that beggar's garment any longer. He already saw himself healed.

Jesus asked Bartimaeus what he wanted Him to do for him, and the beggar replied, ***"Lord, that I might receive my sight."*** Can you see that? He saw with the eye of faith that the sight was already his – "my sight" – it belonged to him. It had been stored up for him already.

He was demanding from Jesus, getting in His face. <u>And he received what he had the faith to demand.</u> ☺

A Personal Testimony – Begging vs. Faith

The Lord taught me about begging early in my ministry, when I was in Minneapolis. It was almost midnight on a Saturday, and I was trying to get a message to preach Sunday morning. I was crying out, "God, I need a message. The people have to have a message." I was bawling and squalling, trying to con God.

I heard a voice say, "What are you doing?" That brought me up short. God asked me how I was to come before Him.

I realized I wasn't acting on what the Word says in Hebrews 4. I wasn't coming ***"boldly before the throne of grace."*** I was begging.

I straightened out my thinking and my asking, and as soon as I did, the sermon started to flow from God into my spirit. I almost couldn't write it down fast enough. Where begging had accomplished nothing, faith and boldness accomplished everything.

I go to different countries preaching faith, and for some reason they seem to think that the God of America is different from the God of Uganda, or the God of Australia, or the God of some other country. I don't know where they got that idea.

I've got to believe for my healing the same way they've got to believe for theirs.

I've got to believe for the money to operate our mall facility the same way they've got to believe for money to run their churches in Costa Rica. I've got to believe for my clothes, my increase, my promotion, everything, just the same way they do over in France.

God is no respecter of persons. Wherever you are, God has put you there so you can demonstrate that <u>in the Kingdom of God there is no lack</u>.

No More Begging Allowed!

That begging mentality is a spirit. You let that thing get on you and you'll always be begging. You'll always want a handout, some welfare, something for nothing from someone else to take care of your needs.

That's just not the way God wants it. He wants you to get your needs met from the inside, by faith.

You've got to stop that begging. Begging not only doesn't work, it sets a sad example for the Kingdom. It makes people think that the Kingdom is broke. The Kingdom is not broke. There's wealth in the Kingdom, but even some pastors don't know it.

They send me letters asking for money. I might be able to help them, but that's not God's best for them. Instead, I send them tapes teaching what I'm telling you here, so they can get what they need for themselves, and not have to ask anybody else.

Instead of begging, stand up for yourself in righteousness, speaking the Word of God. That's what David did when he faced Goliath. He came up to the front line and found all the Israelite soldiers hiding from that giant.

What did David do? David didn't look at Goliath; he looked at God's Word. He had a covenant with almighty God and that ***"uncircumcised Philistine"*** didn't.

David spoke what he knew he had. He dominated Goliath just as he had dominated the lion and the bear when he was a shepherd. David demonstrated the Kingdom in his day.

Now Dominate *Your* Circumstances

Now it's up to us to demonstrate the Kingdom in our day, to manifest the power and the glory of God. Our job is to take back everything that Satan has stolen.

We have the Dominion Mandate to subdue the earth. We've got to start getting some boldness, Saints.

We have to see ourselves the way God sees us. The Word says the righteous (that's us) are as bold as a lion. God will supply your needs just like He will supply mine, every time.

Something to Meditate. We have to do more than speak the way God speaks. We have to think the way God thinks. And that starts with how we think about ourselves. We have to see ourselves as children of the Most High God.

Remember the two blind beggars. Bartimaeus saw himself healed, and he became what he could see. David saw himself as a victor, not just over the lion and the bear, but over Goliath as well. Get the right image of yourself on the inside, and before long that image will manifest on the outside.

CHAPTER THREE

PRACTICING THE GOD-KIND OF FAITH

God is ready to take you further, much further, than your natural mind thinks you can go, because it isn't about your mind. It's about your spirit, being led by His Spirit.

You shouldn't be looking for welfare; you should be expecting to fare well. It's time for the Body of Christ to stop looking like we're something thrown out, orphans with no daddy, just hoping we can get the building fund going and get some old van so we can pick some people up for service because "they ain't got no car."

We have to understand the promises of God with our hearts. Our minds just can't get around them. Our minds are too small and the promises are too big. As it says in Hebrews 10:35-36, ***"Cast not away therefore your confidence, which hath great recompense of reward. For ye have need of patience, that after ye have done the will of God, ye might receive the promise."*** That confidence, or faith, must be in our hearts and it links us to a reward and receiving the promise.

One promise the mind (that's not renewed) has a hard time understanding is that you can have what you say. We never can forget that basic faith scripture in Mark 11:23-24, ***"...whosoever shall say unto this mountain, Be thou removed, and be thou cast into the sea; and shall not doubt in his heart, but shall believe that those things which he saith shall come to pass; he shall have whatsoever he saith. Therefore I say unto you, What things soever ye desire, when ye pray, believe that ye receive them, and ye shall have them."***

That's about the best promise you could have. You do the saying, you do the believing, and God brings it to pass. *great!*

There's no lack in the Kingdom of God. Start thinking like God thinks, because *"as a man thinketh, so is he."*

It's time for the church to get wild for Jesus! Start dominating the devil by keeping the Word of God in your mouth day and night, just like it says in Joshua 1:8, *"This book of the law shall not depart out of thy mouth; but thou shalt meditate therein day and night, that thou mayest observe to do according to all that is written therein: for then thou shalt make thy way prosperous, and then thou shalt have good success."*

When Satan comes to your house, let him have it! Spear him on the end of your sword. Let him know you understand and practice the Dominion Mandate by operating like God, and pretty soon you won't be seeing him around as often. He'll be *"seeking whom he may devour"* somewhere else.

Listen to the Holy Spirit for ways to dominate in every situation. Be bold! Take your city for Jesus! Make a declaration in your church one night. "In the name of Jesus, we're taking this whole city, and devil, you can't stop us. God said we're to dominate the whole earth and that's just what we're going to do."

The church isn't supposed to be in the back of the parade. We're supposed to be the drum majors, the leaders of the parade.

The devil will try to use your relatives and your friends to turn you aside. Don't listen to them. You're going to be like whomever you hang around with, and every morning at 4 o'clock, I start hanging around with Jesus.

Prayer and Faith Work Together

Glory to God! My wife said some time ago, "Sweetheart, people see the <u>results</u> of your hanging around with Jesus, but they don't know how much time you spend in prayer every morning. You need to tell them. Some of them think they just can get up at 8:30, get the newspaper, have a cup of coffee and turn on the TV, and still be powerful for God. It doesn't work that way."

It sure doesn't work that way. To do something great for God, you have to "pray the price." I hit the carpet on my knees in the morning. God gives me a watch. He says, "You've got this watch."

That means I'm responsible for a certain amount of prayer to go forth out of my mouth at a certain hour. I'm responsible for taking Chicago and holding back the forces of evil.

Speaking of holding back, God is not holding anything back from you. He wants to give it to you even more than you want to have it. He is so good.

But you have to do your part. You are His arms, His legs, His feet and His mouth in this hour. If you don't say it, you hold <u>Him</u> back. If you don't go, He can't go. He is depending on you as His ambassador.

God has put us here in these last days. He's depending on us to get the job done, to get His plan accomplished. But we can't do anything without faith.

Faith is not a feeling. Feelings are in the natural realm, not the spiritual realm. As we said before, you can't believe an ounce with your mind; you have to <u>believe</u> with your <u>heart</u>.

Faith Sees Beyond the Senses

Your mind may "believe" in the things you can see, touch, taste, smell, figure out, but that's not faith. Your heart doesn't participate in those things.

But once you get out beyond what your senses can perceive or your mind can reason out, you're in the heart realm, the spirit realm. We can be witnesses to all nations of what the Kingdom of God is really like. Romans 14:17 states, ***"For the kingdom of God is not meat and drink: but righteousness, and peace, and joy in the Holy Ghost."***

When you're walking in faith, God will respond. Jesus didn't stop for Bartimaeus because of his screaming; He stopped because He could see his faith.

Faith connects you to the anointing, and the anointing will remove every burden and destroy every yoke - yokes of lack, yokes of sickness - nothing can withstand the anointing.

You'll begin to see the unseen reality – the heavenly reservoir of blessings that God has stored up for you. And the blessings aren't for you alone. They're to meet the needs of everyone that you know that God has appointed you to bless.

First, you'll have to get your mind and your mouth lined up with the Word of God. As long as you think broke and talk broke, you'll stay broke, no matter how much God wants you to prosper.

Faith Dominates What Appears As Natural

Part of your work in these perilous times is to demonstrate the will of God to those around you. Some of them believe hurricanes and tsunamis are the will of God. When you know and teach what the Word says about storms in Mark 4, you can demolish that idea.

Jesus was crossing the Sea of Galilee with His disciples. He was in the back of the boat sleeping when a fierce storm came up and the waves began filling the boat. The disciples, even though they had been hearing Jesus teach about faith, still became overcome with fear. They awoke Jesus and asked, "Master, don't you care that we're about to die?"

Jesus didn't even bother to answer that foolish question. Instead He took <u>dominion</u>. He <u>rebuked the wind and stopped the storm</u>. Now, if that storm had been God's will, would Jesus have rebuked it? Of course not! The devil had sent that storm to kill Jesus and His disciples.

Folks, including a lot of Christian folks, need to find out what God is really like and what the devil is really like. As we used to say when I was a kid, the devil is very good at "throwing the rock and hiding his hand," so people will blame someone else for what he did.

You'll hear some foolish Christians saying, "Well, God made me sick and put me in the hospital so He could teach me something." No, that's the devil trying to kill you.

Don't fall for his trap. You have authority over him, so take dominion and stop him in his tracks. That's what God expects you to do, not only for your sake, but also for the sake of others who'll notice what you did and learn from it.

When you can testify of how God took away the sickness when you took dominion and spoke His Word, you'll be giving God glory and showing what He is really like.

Taking dominion applies to your finances as well. No way are you supposed to be in lack. You're supposed to be wealthy.

When you exercise dominion by standing on the Word, you'll have *"enough for every good work"* even after all your own needs are met.

Everyone around you - your neighbors and your relatives - should be able to see the blessings of God on your life.

You Must Overcome Unforgiveness

Those neighbors and relatives can be a problem. One thing that can stop you from fulfilling God's plan for you is unforgiveness.

If someone's hurt you, you need to get over it. You have to let it go, because the enemy will play on that. He'll use pride to keep you in unforgiveness. You'll be thinking that because someone owes you something, you're better than they are.

What you need in these last days is faith, not unforgiveness. Unforgiveness will stop your faith from working.

Overcoming unforgiveness includes forgiving people for racism: what "those people" did to me or to "my people." Didn't the Bible say that if you're in the Kingdom you have to love your neighbor? Jesus said that was the second great commandment of the New Covenant, right after loving God. That's all the commandments there are for us, so we'd better keep them!

The damage that fear can cause can't be emphasized enough. Things really are going to look bad in these last times. You can't worry about layoffs. That job isn't your source – God is your source.

Keep your faith on the line and use God's Word to get your needs met. Satan responds to fear the same way God responds to faith. Fear gets Satan moving. He'll try to use fear to pull you back over into the sense realm. Stop him by exercising your dominion, walking in faith, and using the Word.

Something to Meditate. God used His faith to create the world. Abraham used his faith to become the "father of nations." Jesus used His faith to heal the sick, feed multitudes, and raise the dead. And, as it says in Romans, we have that ***"same spirit of faith."***

Develop your faith by spending time in the Word of God. Find promises that apply to what your need is. Keep speaking the promise, not the problem. It will come to pass.

CHAPTER FOUR

YES, YOU CAN DO MIRACLES

Our first job in these last days is spelled out for us by Jesus in Matthew 6:33, ***"But seek ye first the kingdom of God, and his righteousness; and all these things shall be added unto you."***

I am ***"the righteousness of God,"*** and so are you! We're in the God class. I used to kind of shrink back and not say that so boldly because it would upset folks. "You're saying that you're God."

No, I'm a child of God. I have the same attributes as my Father. He doesn't have any problem with me saying that, nor should you. I'm supposed to talk like Him. If He is my father, I am supposed to act like Him.

To act like our Father, we're going to have to start speaking to some storms. We're going to have to start doing things that are supernatural. We are made for the supernatural; as prophesied in Isaiah 8:18, God's children *"are for signs and for wonders."*

Miracles attract everybody, educated and uneducated folks alike, because inside every one of us is a remnant of where we came from and we want to go home.

We want to go back to the supernatural, to where God lives, to the eternal. We have a hunger for it. I know I like miracles – to see someone get up out of a wheelchair or receive a new heart!

God never changes and He's no respecter of persons. It's up to us to "bosom" the promise we need, and to keep saying it until it manifests in our lives.

When you believe and act on the Word, when you know who you really are in Christ and the power that's in His anointing, taking dominion is not that hard. It's not hard to grow a ministry. It's not hard to take a city for God.

The problem is, the church hasn't been following the rules that God laid out. <u>If we come back to doing it God's way, we will see some results that will astound us</u>. There are two scriptures in I and II Peter that will make it clearer.

> ***Blessed be the God and Father of our Lord Jesus Christ, which according to his abundant mercy hath begotten us again unto a lively hope by the resurrection of Jesus Christ from the dead. To an inheritance incorruptible, and undefiled, and that fadeth not away, reserved in heaven for you.***
> ***(I Peter 1:3- 4)***

Although that inheritance is "reserved in heaven for you," it's not talking about when you get there. It's something you can partake of right now.

The second scripture is:

Grace and peace be multiplied unto you through the knowledge of God, and of Jesus our Lord, *(That's revelation knowledge.)* ***According as his divine power hath given unto us all things that pertain unto life and godliness, through the knowledge of him that hath called us to glory and virtue: Whereby are given unto us exceeding great and precious promises: that by these ye might be partakers of the divine nature, having escaped the corruption that is in the world through lust."***

(II Peter 1:2-4)

With revelation knowledge, acting in faith on the precious promises that God has made to us, we can, like the early church in Acts 17:6, again "turn this world upside down."

We especially are to show people the joy of the Lord in the midst of hard times. We believe and live according to Philippians 4:19, *"But my God shall supply all your need according to his riches in glory by Christ Jesus."*

Never forget your inheritance, the things you have received by promise. Hold fast to your profession of faith, and stay in the spirit realm. Don't let the devil drag you back into your flesh. When you go the faith way, nothing can stop you.

We have been ordained, like Esther, for such a time as this. God is ready to take us further than any of us ever have gone in our lives. He loves to see us exercising our Dominion Mandate, dominating the world, the flesh and the devil. So start acting like you're in charge here, because you are!

Something to Meditate. You are the righteous child of a miracle-working God. You were made for signs and wonders and miracles. God believes you can do them. Keep reading and speaking His Word, and you will be doing them.

CONCLUSION

I hope this book has convinced you of the power of God that is in you right now. You were created to operate the same way your Heavenly Father does. As you do, you'll experience more of His spiritual and material blessings in your life. God bless you!

Bill Winston

ABOUT THE AUTHOR

William (Bill) S. Winston is a visionary leader with an insightful awareness of what people need to succeed and how he can empower them for success. Born in Tuskegee, Alabama, Bill credits the strong community and spiritual influences that surrounded him while growing up for the bold determination to be successful and to help others succeed. As a young boy, he was influenced by the courageous examples and historic aviation accomplishments of the Tuskegee Airmen. As a young man, he attended the internationally known Tuskegee Institute (Now Tuskegee University) where the spirit of invention and leadership permeated the environment.

After graduating from Tuskegee Institute, Bill served for six years as a fighter pilot in the United States Air Force, where he received numerous awards and medals for his superior flying skills. His extraordinary achievement in aerial flight earned him The Distinguished Flying Cross, The Air Medal for performance in combat, and Squadron Top Gun Pilot competitions. After completing his military service, Bill joined the IBM Corporation as a marketing representative. His exceptional managerial and relational skills rapidly earned him several promotions within the organization. Before he resigned in 1985 to enter full-time ministry, he was a regional marketing manager in IBM's Midwest Region and was responsible for more than $35 million in sales revenue per year.

Today, Bill Winston is Founder and Pastor of Living Word Christian Center, a 15,000-member church located in Forest Park, Illinois. The church has a broad range of entities including a Bible Training Center, a School of Ministry and Missions, the Joseph Business School, the Forest Park Plaza shopping mall, Living Word Christian Academy, and many others. He also hosts the

Believer's Walk of Faith television and radio broadcast which reaches more than 80 million households nation-wide and overseas.

Pastor Winston is also the Founder and Chairman of The Joseph Center® for Business Development, Chairman of the Board of New Covenant Community Bank (a bank presently in organization), and President of New Covenant Community Development Corporation whose mission is to revitalize communities spiritually and economically.

He is married to Veronica and is the father of three children: Melody, Nicole, and David.

BOOKS BY BILL WINSTON

Born Again and Spirit Filled
Divine Favor
The Power of the Tithe
Power of the Tongue
The Power of Grace
The Spirit of Leadership
Divine Health: A 30-Day Devotional

PRAYER FOR SALVATION AND BAPTISM IN THE HOLY SPIRIT

Heavenly Father, I come to You in the Name of Your Son Jesus Christ. You said in Your Word that whosoever shall call upon the Name of the Lord shall be saved (Romans 10:13). Father, I am calling on Jesus right now. I believe He died on the cross for my sins, that He was raised from the dead on the third day, and He's alive right now. Lord Jesus, I am asking You now, come into my heart. Live Your life in me and through me. I repent of my sins and surrender myself totally and completely to You. Heavenly Father, by faith I now confess Jesus Christ as my new Lord and Savior from this day forward, I dedicate my life to serving Him.

BILL WINSTON MINISTRIES

We'd like to hear from you!

Please send us your prayer request or praise report. For more information about Bill Winston Ministries and a free product catalog, please write to us or visit us on the worldwide web at:

Bill Winston Ministries
P.O. Box 947
Oak Park, Illinois 60303-0947
(708) 697-5100
(800) 711-9327

www.bwm.org

TO RECEIVE THE INFILLING OF THE HOLY SPIRIT

My Heavenly Father, I am Your child, for I believe in my heart that Jesus has been raised from the dead and I have confessed Him as my Lord.

Jesus said, "How much more shall your heavenly Father give the Holy Spirit to those who ask Him." I ask You now in the Name of Jesus to fill me with the Holy Spirit. I step into the fullness and power that I desire in the Name of Jesus. I confess that I am a Spirit-filled Christian. As I yield my vocal organs, I expect to speak in tongues for the Spirit gives me utterance in the Name of Jesus. Praise the Lord! Amen.

Scripture References:

John 14:16-17
Luke 11:13
Acts 1:8a
Acts 2:4
Acts 2:32-33, 39
Acts 8:12-17
Acts 10:44-46
Acts 19:2, 5-6
1 Corinthians 14:2-15
1 Corinthians 14:18, 27
Ephesians 6:18
Jude 1:20